cooking for le$$
Ground Beef

Publications International, Ltd.

Favorite Brand Name Recipes at www.fbnr.com

Microwave Cooking: Microwave ovens vary in wattage. Use the cooking times as guidelines and check for doneness before adding more time.

Preparation/Cooking Times: Preparation times are based on the approximate amount of time required to assemble the recipe before cooking, baking, chilling or serving. These times include preparation steps such as measuring, chopping and mixing. The fact that some preparations and cooking can be done simultaneously is taken into account. Preparation of optional ingredients and serving suggestions is not included.

contents

Cutting back on your food bill shouldn't mean depriving yourself. With the recipes in this book and a few tips, you can eat better for less.

Supermarket Savvy

Think about the week ahead before you go shopping. Will half the family be home too late for dinner on Wednesday night? Will Thursday be so busy that you need to plan something extra quick and stress free? Jotting down the kinds of meals you'll need can save you from buying too much. Then make a grocery list and stick to it. It's easier to resist the colorful displays if you're prepared. It also helps to shop alone if possible, and it goes without saying that you should never, ever grocery shop when you're hungry!

Supermarkets are designed to get you to spend! Items are arranged so that you'll see enticing assortments of not-so-necessary goodies on your way to buy the milk and bread. Stick to the perimeter of the store as much as possible. That's where meat, produce and dairy are usually stocked. Read the sale flyers ahead of time while you're planning, and don't forget to bring along the coupons.

Beware of Bargains That Aren't

Do remember that the best price in the world on chicken livers isn't going to convince your family to eat them. Buying big, bargain sizes of items you know you'll use makes sense, but check the label posted on the shelf under the product. A giant economy size may look like a good deal, but sometimes it isn't. The small print listing cost per ounce may surprise you.

Healthy Budgeting

The good news is that eating more fruits and vegetables and less meat is better for your health as well as your wallet. Instead of just concentrating on meat as the centerpiece of a meal, consider what will go with it. You can stretch smaller portions of expensive protein with pasta, grains, rice and side dishes. You can take some cues from ethnic cooks, too. Asian dishes often use a small amount of chicken or beef to flavor a stir-fry that's mostly vegetables. Mexican cuisine counts on tortillas, rice and beans. Italians have pasta and pizza.

Add Flavor Instead of Dollars

Herbs and spices cost a lot per jar, but they can add huge amounts of flavor for only pennies. A little bit of mustard, balsamic vinegar or hot sauce can turn boring into mouthwatering. Stock up on flavorful pantry ingredients like these and you'll have lots of delicious options every time you cook.

Waste Less, Spend Less

Most of us end up discarding too much of the food we buy. (According to a government study, Americans waste one pound of food per day on average.) Think about what category your discards fall into and see if you can improve. Are you tossing vegetables that have rotted? Maybe you can shop more often or use frozen or canned. The kids don't clean their plates? Serve smaller portions and you can always refill them. You planned on making dinner, but life got in the way? You may be able to freeze ingredients or use them another way.

Pat Yourself on the Back

Cooking at home more and eating out less is a huge step in the right direction. It almost always saves money and provides more nutritious meals for your family. With a little creativity and planning, cooking for less can also be a delicious undertaking— and that's the best bargain of all!

FIESTA BEEF ENCHILADAS

- 6 ounces ground beef
- ¼ cup sliced green onions
- 1 clove garlic, minced
- 1 cup (4 ounces) shredded Mexican cheese blend or Cheddar cheese, divided
- ¾ cup chopped tomato, divided
- ½ cup cooked rice
- ½ cup frozen corn, thawed
- ½ cup black beans
- ¼ cup salsa or picante sauce
- 6 (6-inch) corn tortillas
- ½ cup red or green enchilada sauce
- ½ cup shredded romaine lettuce

1. Preheat oven to 375°F. Spray medium baking dish with nonstick cooking spray.

2. Brown beef in large skillet over medium-high heat, stirring to break up meat. Drain fat. Add green onions and garlic; cook and stir 2 minutes.

3. Combine beef mixture, ¾ cup cheese, ½ cup tomato, rice, corn, beans and salsa; mix well. Spoon mixture down center of tortillas. Roll up tortillas; place seam side down in prepared baking dish. Spread enchilada sauce evenly over tortillas.

4. Bake 15 minutes. Sprinkle with remaining ¼ cup cheese; bake 10 minutes. Serve with lettuce and remaining ¼ cup tomato.

Makes 2 servings

HEARTY SHEPHERD'S PIE

1½ pounds ground beef
2 cups *French's*® French Fried Onions
1 can (10¾ ounces) condensed tomato soup
½ cup water
2 teaspoons Italian seasoning
¼ teaspoon *each* salt and black pepper
1 package (10 ounces) frozen mixed vegetables, thawed
3 cups hot mashed potatoes

1. Preheat oven to 375°F. Cook meat in large ovenproof skillet until browned; drain. Stir in *1 cup* French Fried Onions, soup, water, seasoning, salt and pepper.

2. Spoon vegetables over beef mixture. Top with mashed potatoes.

3. Bake 20 minutes or until hot. Sprinkle with remaining *1 cup* onions. Bake 2 minutes or until golden.   *Makes 6 servings*

Prep Time: 10 minutes
Cook Time: 27 minutes

Store ground beef in the coldest part of the refrigerator for up to two days, making sure it is well wrapped and set on the lowest shelf to avoid dripping on any other foods. Ground beef can also be tightly wrapped and frozen for up to three months.

TACO SALAD SUPREME

 1 pound ground beef
½ cup chopped onion
 2 cloves garlic, minced
 1 teaspoon ground cumin
 1 teaspoon chili powder
½ teaspoon salt
½ cup salsa, divided
 6 cups packed torn or sliced romaine lettuce
 1 large tomato, chopped
 1 cup (4 ounces) shredded Mexican cheese blend or
    taco cheese, divided
 2 tablespoons canola oil
 1 ripe avocado, diced (optional)
¼ cup sour cream

1. Cook beef and onion in large skillet over medium-high heat 6 to
8 minutes, stirring to break up meat. Drain fat. Add garlic, cumin,
chili powder and salt; cook 1 minute, stirring frequently. Stir in
¼ cup salsa; cook and stir 1 minute. Remove from heat.

2. Combine lettuce, tomato and ½ cup cheese in large bowl.
Combine remaining ¼ cup salsa and oil in small bowl. Add
salsa mixture to salad; toss to coat.

3. Divide salad among 4 serving plates. Spoon beef mixture
evenly over salad; top with remaining ½ cup cheese, avocado,
if desired, and sour cream.

Makes 4 servings

MAMA'S BEST EVER SPAGHETTI & MEATBALLS

     1 pound lean ground beef
     ½ cup Italian seasoned dry bread crumbs
     1 egg
     1 jar (1 pound 10 ounces) RAGÚ® Old World Style® Pasta Sauce
     8 ounces spaghetti, cooked and drained

1. In medium bowl, combine ground beef, bread crumbs and egg; shape into 12 meatballs.

2. In 3-quart saucepan, bring Ragú Pasta Sauce to a boil over medium-high heat. Gently stir in meatballs.

3. Reduce heat to low and simmer covered, stirring occasionally, 20 minutes or until meatballs are no longer pink in center. Serve over hot spaghetti; sprinkle with shredded Parmesan cheese, if desired.

Makes 4 servings

ZESTY ONION MEATLOAF

     2 pounds ground beef
  1⅓ cups *French's*® French Fried Onions
     1 cup spaghetti sauce, divided
     ½ cup bread crumbs
     ¼ cup *French's*® Worcestershire Sauce
     2 eggs

1. Preheat oven to 350°F. Thoroughly mix beef, ⅔ *cup* French Fried Onions, ½ *cup* sauce, bread crumbs, Worcestershire Sauce and eggs in large bowl.

2. Shape into loaf in baking dish. Bake 1 hour or until thoroughly cooked and internal temperature reaches 160°F; drain. Top with remaining ½ *cup* sauce and ⅔ *cup* onions. Bake 5 minutes or until onions are golden.

Makes 6 to 8 servings

BEEF & ZUCCHINI QUICHE

  1 unbaked 9-inch pie crust
½ pound ground beef
  1 medium zucchini, shredded
  3 green onions, sliced
¼ cup sliced mushrooms
  1 tablespoon all-purpose flour
  1 cup milk
  3 eggs, beaten
¾ cup (3 ounces) shredded Swiss cheese
½ teaspoon dried thyme *or* 1½ teaspoons chopped fresh thyme
½ teaspoon salt
    Dash black pepper
    Dash ground red pepper

1. Preheat oven to 475°F.

2. Line pie crust with foil; fill with dried beans, rice or pie weights. Bake 8 minutes. Remove from oven; carefully remove foil and beans. Return pie crust to oven; bake 4 minutes. *Reduce oven temperature to 375°F.*

3. Brown beef in medium skillet over medium-high heat, stirring to break up meat. Drain fat. Add zucchini, green onions and mushrooms; cook, stirring occasionally, until vegetables are tender. Stir in flour; cook 2 minutes, stirring constantly. Remove from heat.

4. Combine milk, eggs, cheese, thyme, salt, black pepper and red pepper in medium bowl; stir into beef mixture. Pour filling into crust.

5. Bake 35 minutes or until knife inserted near center comes out clean.

Makes 6 servings

beef & zucchini quiche

TEX–MEX MEATLOAF

   2 tablespoons olive oil
   1 teaspoon POLANER® Chopped Garlic
   1 onion, diced
   2 tablespoons ORTEGA® Diced Green Chiles
   1 ORTEGA® Two Cheese Grande Pizza Kit—includes 10 tostada shells,
       1 packet (1.25 ounces) taco seasoning mix, 1 packet (3 ounces)
       taco sauce and 1 packet each LAND O LAKES® Mozzarella and
       Nacho Cheese Sauce
   2 pounds meatloaf mix (ground beef, ground pork and veal) or lean
       ground beef
   2 eggs
   ½ cup milk
   2 tablespoons Worcestershire sauce
   1 teaspoon dried oregano
   ½ cup ORTEGA® Taco Sauce
   2 tablespoons brown sugar
   1 tablespoon REGINA® Red Wine Vinegar

Preheat oven to 350°F. Heat olive oil in skillet over medium-high heat until hot. Add garlic, onion and chiles. Cook and stir until onions are browned, about 4 minutes.

Process 10 tostada shells from Pizza Kit in blender or food processor to make crumbs equal to about 1 cup (or place tostadas in plastic bag and roll with heavy rolling pin to make crumbs).

Combine onion mixture, ground tostadas, meat, eggs, milk, Worcestershire sauce and oregano in large bowl. Add Mozzarella Cheese packet, taco sauce packet and seasoning mix from Pizza Kit.* Mix well. Form into small football-shaped mound. Place on well-oiled rack over baking sheet (or place on foiled-lined baking sheet or in 1½-quart meatloaf pan).

Make basting sauce by combining ½ cup taco sauce with brown sugar and vinegar in small bowl. Brush meatloaf with basting sauce before placing in oven. Bake meatloaf 1 hour, basting with sauce every 15 minutes. Let meatloaf rest 5 minutes before cutting and serving.

Makes 6 servings

Use the Nacho Cheese Sauce from the Pizza Kit as a dipping sauce, or heat and serve as a cheese gravy.

ITALIAN–STYLE MEATBALL SOUP

½ pound ground beef
¼ pound ground Italian sausage
1 large onion, finely chopped, divided
⅓ cup dry bread crumbs
1 egg
½ teaspoon salt
4 cups reduced-sodium beef broth
2 cups water
1 can (8 ounces) stewed tomatoes
1 can (8 ounces) pizza sauce
2 cups sliced cabbage
1 can (about 15 ounces) kidney beans, drained
2 medium carrots, sliced
½ cup frozen Italian green beans

1. Combine beef, sausage, 2 tablespoons onion, bread crumbs, egg and salt in large bowl; mix until well blended. Shape into 32 (1-inch) meatballs.

2. Brown half of meatballs in large skillet over medium heat, turning frequently and shaking skillet to evenly brown meatballs. Remove from skillet; drain meatballs on paper towels. Repeat with remaining meatballs.

3. Bring broth, water, tomatoes and pizza sauce to a boil in Dutch oven over high heat. Add meatballs, remaining onion, cabbage, beans and carrots; bring to a boil. Reduce heat; simmer, uncovered, 20 minutes. Add green beans; return to a boil. Reduce heat; simmer, uncovered, 10 minutes. *Makes 8 servings*

EMPANADA PIE

    1 tablespoon vegetable oil
    1 small onion, chopped
    1 pound ground beef
    1 package (1¼ ounces) taco seasoning mix
    1 can (8 ounces) tomato sauce
    ¼ cup raisins
    2 teaspoons dark brown sugar
    1 package refrigerated crescent roll dough (8 rolls)
      Sliced green onion (optional)

1. Preheat oven to 375°F. Grease 10-inch shallow round baking dish or deep-dish pie plate.

2. Heat oil in large skillet over medium-high heat. Add onion; cook 2 to 3 minutes or until translucent. Add beef; brown 6 to 8 minutes, stirring to break up meat. Drain fat. Sprinkle taco seasoning over beef mixture. Add tomato sauce, raisins and brown sugar. Reduce heat to low; cook 2 to 3 minutes.

3. Spoon beef mixture into prepared dish. Unroll crescent dough; separate into triangles. Arrange 5 triangles on top of beef mixture in a spiral with points of dough towards center. Reserve remaining dough for another use. Do not seal dough pieces together.

4. Bake 13 to 17 minutes or until dough is puffed and golden brown. Garnish with green onion. *Makes 4 to 6 servings*

SALSA BEEF SALAD

     1 pound ground beef
     1 can (about 15 ounces) pinto beans, rinsed and drained
     2 jalapeño peppers,* seeded and chopped
     2 tablespoons chili powder
     ½ teaspoon ground cumin
       Salt and black pepper
     1 head iceberg lettuce, shredded
     2 medium tomatoes, diced
     ½ cup shredded pepper jack cheese
     ¼ cup chopped fresh cilantro
     ½ cup chopped green onions
       Juice of 1 lime
     1 cup salsa
     1 package (12 ounces) corn tortilla chips, broken
       Sour cream (optional)

Jalapeño peppers can sting and irritate the skin, so wear rubber gloves when handling peppers and do not touch your eyes.

1. Brown beef in large skillet over medium-high heat, stirring to break up meat. Drain fat.

2. Add beans, jalapeños, chili powder, cumin, salt and pepper to skillet; cook and stir 5 minutes or until heated through. Set aside to cool.

3. Combine lettuce, tomatoes, cheese and cilantro in large bowl. Top with beef mixture, green onions and lime juice. Serve with salsa, chips and sour cream, if desired. *Makes 4 to 6 servings*

SIMPLE SALISBURY STEAK

     1 pound ground beef
     1 can (10¾ ounces) CAMPBELL'S® Condensed Cream of Mushroom Soup
          (Regular or 98% Fat Free)
     ⅓ cup dry bread crumbs
     1 egg, beaten
     1 small onion, finely chopped (about ¼ cup)
     1 tablespoon vegetable oil
     1½ cups sliced mushrooms

1. Thoroughly mix the beef, **¼ cup** of the soup, bread crumbs, egg and onion in a medium bowl. Shape the mixture into 4 (½-inch thick) burgers.

2. Heat the oil in a 10-inch skillet over medium-high heat. Add the burgers and cook until well browned on both sides. Remove the burgers with a slotted spatula and set aside.

3. Stir the remaining soup and mushrooms into the skillet. Heat to a boil. Return the burgers to the skillet and reduce the heat to low. Cover and cook for 10 minutes or until the burgers are cooked through.*

Makes 4 servings

**The internal temperature of the burgers should reach 160°F.*

Time-Saving Tip: To speed up meal preparation, do some of the work ahead. Shape the burgers, cover and refrigerate. You can also save time by purchasing chopped onions and sliced mushrooms.

simple salisbury steak

FAMILY–STYLE BEEF PIZZA

   1 package (about 14 ounces) refrigerated pizza dough
   ¼ pound ground beef
   ½ cup chopped green bell pepper
   3 tablespoons finely chopped onion
   ¾ cup pizza sauce
   1 small tomato, peeled, seeded and chopped
   2 teaspoons Italian seasoning
   2 cloves garlic, minced
   ⅛ teaspoon ground red pepper
   ½ cup sliced mushrooms
   1 cup (4 ounces) shredded mozzarella cheese
   2 tablespoons grated Parmesan cheese

1. Preheat oven to 425°F. Lightly spray 12-inch pizza pan with nonstick cooking spray. Unroll pizza dough; press into prepared pan. Build up edges slightly. Prick dough all over with fork. Bake 7 to 10 minutes or until lightly browned.

2. Cook beef, bell pepper and onion in large skillet over medium-high heat 4 to 6 minutes, stirring to break up meat. Drain fat.

3. Combine pizza sauce, tomato, Italian seasoning, garlic and red pepper in small saucepan over medium heat; bring to a boil. Reduce heat; simmer, uncovered, about 8 minutes or until desired consistency.

4. Spread tomato mixture evenly over pizza crust. Sprinkle with beef mixture and mushrooms. Sprinkle with cheeses. Bake 5 to 8 minutes or until heated through.

Makes 6 servings

Prep Time: 20 minutes
Bake Time: 12 to 18 minutes

CLASSIC BEEF STROGANOFF

    1 cup MINUTE® White Rice, uncooked
    1 tablespoon vegetable oil
    1 cup chopped onion
    1 pound lean ground beef
    2 cups sliced mushrooms
    1 can (14½ ounces) beef broth
    1 tablespoon Worcestershire sauce
    1 can (10¾ ounces) cream of mushroom soup
    ½ cup sour cream

Prepare rice according to package directions. Heat oil in medium skillet over medium-high heat. Add onion; cook and stir 3 minutes. Add beef and brown; drain excess fat. Add mushrooms, broth, Worcestershire sauce and soup. Bring to a boil and simmer 5 minutes. Stir in sour cream. Serve over rice. *Makes 4 servings*

EASY BEEF LASAGNA

    1 pound ground beef
    1 jar (1 pound 10 ounces) RAGÚ® Old World Style® Pasta Sauce
    1 container (15 ounces) ricotta cheese
    2 cups shredded mozzarella cheese (about 8 ounces)
    ½ cup grated Parmesan cheese
    2 eggs
   12 lasagna noodles, cooked and drained

1. Preheat oven to 375°F. In 12-inch skillet, brown ground beef; drain. Stir in Ragú Pasta Sauce; heat through. In large bowl, combine ricotta cheese, mozzarella cheese, ¼ cup Parmesan cheese and eggs.

2. In 13×9-inch baking dish, spread 1 cup meat sauce. Arrange 4 lasagna noodles lengthwise over sauce, then 1 cup meat sauce and ½ of ricotta mixture. Repeat, ending with sauce. Cover with aluminum foil and bake 30 minutes. Sprinkle with remaining ¼ cup Parmesan. Bake uncovered 5 minutes. Let stand 10 minutes before serving. *Makes 10 servings*

PASTITSIO

   8 ounces uncooked ziti or elbow macaroni
   1 pound ground beef
   ½ cup chopped onion
   1 clove garlic, finely chopped
   1 can (8 ounces) tomato sauce
   ½ teaspoon dried oregano
   ½ teaspoon black pepper
   ¼ teaspoon ground cinnamon
   2 tablespoons butter
   2 tablespoons all-purpose flour
 1½ cups milk
   1 egg, beaten
   1 cup grated Parmesan cheese, divided

1. Preheat oven to 350°F. Spray 9-inch baking dish with nonstick cooking spray.

2. Cook pasta according to package directions. Drain and set aside.

3. Cook and stir beef, onion and garlic in large skillet over medium-high heat until beef is no longer pink. Drain fat. Stir in tomato sauce, oregano, pepper and cinnamon. Reduce heat to low; simmer 10 minutes.

4. Spread half of pasta in prepared dish. Top with beef mixture, then remaining pasta.

5. For sauce, melt butter in medium saucepan. Stir in flour; cook and stir 1 minute. Whisk in milk; cook 6 minutes, stirring constantly, until thickened. Stir some of sauce into egg. Return egg mixture to saucepan; cook and stir 2 minutes. Stir in ¾ cup cheese.

6. Pour sauce mixture over top pasta layer. Sprinkle with remaining ¼ cup cheese. Bake 30 to 40 minutes or until heated through and golden brown.

Makes 6 servings

CRUNCHY LAYERED BEEF & BEAN SALAD

    1 pound ground beef or turkey
    2 cans (15 to 19 ounces each) black beans or pinto beans, rinsed and
        drained
    1 can (14½ ounces) stewed tomatoes, undrained
 1⅓ cups *French's*® French Fried Onions, divided
    1 tablespoon *Frank's*® *RedHot*® Original Cayenne Pepper Sauce
    1 package (1¼ ounces) taco seasoning mix
    6 cups shredded lettuce
    1 cup (4 ounces) shredded Cheddar or Monterey Jack cheese

1. Cook beef in large nonstick skillet over medium heat until thoroughly browned; drain well. Stir in beans, tomatoes, ⅔ *cup* French Fried Onions, **Frank's RedHot** Sauce and taco seasoning. Heat to boiling. Cook over medium heat 5 minutes, stirring occasionally.

2. Spoon beef mixture over lettuce on serving platter. Top with cheese.

3. Microwave remaining ⅔ *cup* onions 1 minute on HIGH. Sprinkle over salad.   *Makes 6 servings*

Prep Time: 10 minutes
Cook Time: 6 minutes

To save money at the grocery store, purchase blocks of cheese instead of packages of pre-shredded cheese. Use a hand grater or a food processor, and make sure that semifirm cheeses such as Cheddar and Monterey Jack are cold to make grating the cheese easier.

crunchy layered beef & bean salad

comforting casseroles

LAYERED PASTA CASSEROLE

  8 ounces uncooked penne pasta
½ pound mild Italian sausage, casings removed
½ pound ground beef
  1 jar (about 26 ounces) pasta sauce
  1 package (10 ounces) frozen chopped spinach, thawed and
      squeezed dry
  1 cup ricotta cheese
  2 cups (8 ounces) shredded mozzarella cheese, divided
½ cup grated Parmesan cheese
  1 egg
  2 tablespoons chopped fresh basil *or* 2 teaspoons dried basil
  1 teaspoon salt

1. Preheat oven to 350°F. Spray 13×9-inch baking dish with nonstick cooking spray. Cook pasta according to package directions; drain. Transfer to prepared dish.

2. Meanwhile, brown sausage and beef in large skillet over medium-high heat, stirring to break up meat. Drain fat. Add pasta sauce; mix well. Add half of meat sauce to pasta; toss to coat.

3. Combine spinach, ricotta, 1 cup mozzarella, Parmesan, egg, basil and salt in medium bowl. Spoon small mounds of spinach mixture over pasta mixture; spread evenly with back of spoon. Top with remaining meat sauce; sprinkle with remaining 1 cup mozzarella. Bake, uncovered, 30 minutes. *Makes 6 to 8 servings*

CAJUN–STYLE BEEF AND BEANS

       1 pound ground beef
     ¾ cup chopped onion
    2½ cups cooked rice
       1 can (about 15 ounces) kidney beans, rinsed and drained
       1 can (about 14 ounces) stewed tomatoes
       2 teaspoons Cajun seasoning or to taste
     ¾ cup (3 ounces) shredded Cheddar cheese

1. Preheat oven to 350°F. Brown beef in large skillet over medium-high heat, stirring to break up meat. Drain fat. Add onion to skillet; cook and stir 3 to 5 minutes or until onion is translucent.

2. Combine beef mixture, rice, beans, tomatoes and Cajun seasoning in 2- to 2½-quart casserole.

3. Bake, covered, 25 to 30 minutes, stirring once during baking. Remove from oven; sprinkle with cheese. Let stand, covered, 5 minutes before serving. *Makes 6 servings*

Tip: To prepare your own Cajun seasoning, place 5 tablespoons ground red pepper, 3 tablespoons black pepper, 3 tablespoons onion powder, 3 tablespoons garlic powder, 3 tablespoons chili powder, 1 tablespoon dried thyme, 1 tablespoon dried basil or parsley flakes and 1 tablespoon ground bay leaf in a blender. Blend until spices are well combined. If desired, stir in ½ cup salt by hand. Store in a tightly sealed container.

cajun-style beef and beans

NO–CHOP PASTITSIO

       1 pound ground beef
    1½ cups mild picante sauce
       1 can (8 ounces) tomato sauce
       1 tablespoon sugar
       ½ teaspoon ground allspice
       ½ teaspoon ground cinnamon
       ¼ teaspoon ground nutmeg, divided
       8 ounces uncooked elbow macaroni
       3 tablespoons butter
       3 tablespoons all-purpose flour
    1½ cups milk
       ½ teaspoon salt
       ¼ teaspoon black pepper
       2 eggs, beaten
       ½ cup grated Parmesan cheese

1. Preheat oven to 350°F. Lightly spray 9-inch square baking dish with nonstick cooking spray.

2. Brown beef in large skillet over medium-high heat, stirring to break up meat. Drain fat. Add picante sauce, tomato sauce, sugar, allspice, cinnamon and ⅛ teaspoon nutmeg. Bring to a boil; reduce heat and simmer, uncovered, 10 minutes, stirring frequently.

3. Meanwhile, cook macaroni according to package directions; drain. Place in prepared baking dish.

4. Melt butter in medium saucepan over medium heat. Add flour; mix until smooth. Add milk; cook and stir until thickened. Remove from heat. Add about ½ cup white sauce to eggs; stir to blend thoroughly. Add egg mixture to remaining white sauce in saucepan. Stir in cheese.

5. Stir about ½ cup white sauce into macaroni; toss to coat completely. Spread meat sauce over macaroni. Top with remaining white sauce. Sprinkle with remaining ⅛ teaspoon nutmeg. Bake, uncovered, 30 to 40 minutes or until knife inserted into center comes out clean. Let stand 15 to 20 minutes before serving. *Makes 6 servings*

no-chop pastitsio

QUICK TACO MACARONI & CHEESE

- 1 pound lean ground beef or turkey
- 1 package (1 ounce) LAWRY'S® Taco Spices & Seasonings
- 1 package (1 pound) large elbow macaroni, cooked and drained
- 4 cups (16 ounces) shredded Cheddar cheese
- 2 cups milk
- 3 eggs, beaten

In medium skillet, brown ground meat; drain fat. Stir in Taco Spices & Seasonings. Spray 13×9×2-inch baking dish with nonstick cooking spray. Layer half of macaroni in bottom of dish. Top with half of cheese. Spread taco meat over top and repeat layers of macaroni and cheese. In medium bowl, beat together milk and eggs. Pour egg mixture over top of casserole. Bake in preheated 350°F oven for 30 to 35 minutes or until golden brown. *Makes 6 to 8 servings*

Variation: For spicier flavor, try using LAWRY'S® Chili Spices & Seasonings or LAWRY'S® Hot Taco Spices & Seasonings instead of Taco Spices & Seasonings.

Pasta that is to be baked in a casserole should be slightly undercooked. If it is prepared according to the package directions, it will become too soft and will fall apart after baking.

BEEF & ARTICHOKE CASSEROLE

¾ **pound ground beef**
½ **cup sliced mushrooms**
¼ **cup chopped onion**
 1 **clove garlic, minced**
 1 **can (14 ounces) artichoke hearts, drained and chopped**
½ **cup dry bread crumbs**
½ **cup grated Parmesan cheese**
 1 **teaspoon dried rosemary** *or* **1 tablespoon chopped fresh rosemary**
½ **teaspoon dried marjoram** *or* **1½ teaspoons chopped fresh marjoram**
   Salt and black pepper
 3 **egg whites**

1. Preheat oven to 400°F. Spray 1-quart casserole with nonstick cooking spray.

2. Brown beef in medium skillet over medium-high heat, stirring to break up meat. Drain fat. Add mushrooms, onion and garlic; cook and stir until tender.

3. Combine beef mixture, artichokes, bread crumbs, cheese, rosemary and marjoram; mix lightly. Season with salt and pepper.

4. Beat egg whites in medium bowl with electric mixer at high speed until stiff peaks form; fold into beef mixture. Spoon into prepared casserole.

5. Bake 20 minutes or until lightly browned around edges.

Makes 4 servings

SPINACH–POTATO BAKE

    1 pound ground beef
    1 small onion, chopped
    ½ cup sliced mushrooms
    2 cloves garlic, minced
    1 package (10 ounces) frozen chopped spinach, thawed and well
        drained
    ½ teaspoon ground nutmeg
    1 pound russet potatoes, peeled, cooked and mashed
    ¼ cup sour cream
    ¼ cup milk
      Salt and black pepper
    ½ cup (2 ounces) shredded Cheddar cheese

1. Preheat oven to 400°F. Spray deep 9-inch casserole with nonstick cooking spray.

2. Brown beef in large skillet over medium-high heat, stirring to break up meat. Drain fat. Add onion, mushrooms and garlic; cook and stir until tender. Stir in spinach and nutmeg; cook until heated through, stirring occasionally.

3. Combine potatoes, sour cream and milk. Add to beef mixture; season with salt and pepper. Spoon into prepared casserole; sprinkle with cheese.

4. Bake 15 to 20 minutes or until slightly puffed and cheese is melted.

Makes 6 servings

spinach-potato bake

MIDWEEK MOUSSAKA

    1 eggplant (about 1 pound), cut into ¼-inch slices
    2 tablespoons olive oil
    1 pound ground beef
    1 can (about 14 ounces) stewed tomatoes, drained
    ¼ cup red wine
    2 tablespoons tomato paste
    2 teaspoons sugar
    ¾ teaspoon salt
    ½ teaspoon dried oregano
    ¼ teaspoon ground cinnamon
    ¼ teaspoon black pepper
    ⅛ teaspoon ground allspice
    4 ounces cream cheese
    ¼ cup milk
    ¼ cup grated Parmesan cheese
      Additional ground cinnamon (optional)

1. Preheat broiler. Spray 8-inch square baking dish with nonstick cooking spray. Line baking sheet with foil. Arrange eggplant slices on foil, overlapping slightly if necessary. Brush with oil; broil 5 to 6 inches from heat source 4 minutes on each side. *Reduce oven temperature to 350°F.*

2. Meanwhile, brown beef in large skillet over medium-high heat, stirring to break up meat. Drain fat. Add tomatoes, wine, tomato paste, sugar, salt, oregano, cinnamon, pepper and allspice. Bring to a boil, breaking up large pieces of tomato with spoon. Reduce heat to medium-low; simmer, covered, 10 minutes.

3. Place cream cheese and milk in small microwavable bowl; cover. Microwave on HIGH 1 minute; stir until smooth.

4. Arrange half of eggplant slices in prepared baking dish. Spoon half of meat sauce over eggplant; sprinkle with half of Parmesan. Repeat layers. Spoon cream cheese mixture evenly on top. Bake 20 minutes or until top begins to crack slightly. Sprinkle lightly with cinnamon, if desired. Let stand 10 minutes before serving. *Makes 4 servings*

SLOPPY JOE CASSEROLE

 1 **pound ground beef**
 1 **can (10¾ ounces) CAMPBELL'S® Condensed Tomato Soup**
¼ **cup water**
 1 **teaspoon Worcestershire sauce**
⅛ **teaspoon ground black pepper**
 1 **package (7.5 ounces) refrigerated biscuits (10 biscuits)**
½ **cup shredded Cheddar cheese**

1. Cook the beef in a 10-inch skillet over medium-high heat until the beef is well browned, stirring frequently to break up meat. Pour off any fat.

2. Stir the soup, water, Worcestershire and black pepper into the skillet. Heat to a boil. Spoon the beef mixture into a 1½-quart casserole. Arrange the biscuits over the beef mixture around the edge of the casserole.

3. Bake at 400°F. for 15 minutes or until the biscuits are golden brown. Sprinkle the cheese over the beef mixture. *Makes 5 servings*

Prep Time: 10 minutes
Bake Time: 15 minutes

BAKED BLACK BEAN CHILI

1½ pounds ground beef
¼ cup chopped onion
¼ cup chopped green bell pepper
1 can (about 15 ounces) black beans, rinsed and drained
1 can (about 14 ounces) diced tomatoes with green chilies
1 can (about 14 ounces) beef broth
1 can (8 ounces) tomato sauce
¼ cup plus 1 tablespoon chili powder
1 tablespoon sugar
1 tablespoon ground cumin
1 teaspoon dried minced onion
⅛ teaspoon garlic powder
⅛ teaspoon ground ginger
2 cups (8 ounces) shredded Mexican cheese blend

1. Preheat oven to 350°F. Cook beef, onion and pepper in large skillet over medium-high heat 6 to 8 minutes, stirring to break up meat. Drain fat. Transfer to 4-quart casserole.

2. Stir in beans, tomatoes, broth, tomato sauce, chili powder, sugar, cumin, dried onion, garlic powder and ginger.

3. Bake, covered, 30 minutes, stirring every 10 minutes. Sprinkle with cheese; bake, covered, about 5 minutes or until cheese begins to melt.

Makes 6 to 8 servings

baked black bean chili

51

ITALIAN–STYLE SHEPHERD'S PIE

     1 pound potatoes, peeled and quartered
     2 to 3 tablespoons reduced-sodium chicken broth
    ¼ cup grated Parmesan cheese
     1 pound ground beef
    ½ cup chopped onion
     2 teaspoons Italian seasoning
    ¼ teaspoon fennel seeds, finely crushed (optional)
    ⅛ teaspoon ground red pepper
     2 cups sliced yellow summer squash
     1 can (about 14 ounces) chunky pasta-style tomatoes, drained
     1 cup frozen corn
    ⅓ cup tomato paste

1. Preheat oven to 375°F. Combine potatoes and enough water to cover in medium saucepan. Bring to a boil. Boil, uncovered, 20 to 25 minutes or until tender; drain. Mash potatoes, adding enough broth to reach desired consistency. Stir in cheese. Set aside.

2. Cook beef and onion in large skillet over medium-high heat 6 to 8 minutes, stirring to break up meat. Drain fat. Stir in Italian seasoning, fennel seeds, if desired, and red pepper. Add squash, tomatoes, corn and tomato paste; mix well. Spoon mixture into 2-quart casserole. Pipe or spoon potatoes over top of casserole.

3. Bake 20 to 25 minutes or until meat mixture is bubbly. Let stand 10 minutes before serving. *Makes 6 servings*

Prep Time: 30 minutes
Bake Time: 20 minutes

italian-style shepherd's pie

MEXICAN LASAGNA

   1 jar (1 pound 10 ounces) RAGÚ® Old World Style® Pasta Sauce
   1 pound ground beef
   1 can (15¼ ounces) whole kernel corn, drained
  4½ teaspoons chili powder
   6 (8½-inch) flour tortillas
   2 cups shredded Cheddar cheese (about 8 ounces)

1. Preheat oven to 350°F. Set aside 1 cup Ragú Pasta Sauce. In 10-inch skillet, brown ground beef over medium-high heat; drain. Stir in remaining Ragú Pasta Sauce, corn and chili powder.

2. In 13×9-inch baking dish, spread 1 cup sauce mixture. Arrange two tortillas over sauce, overlapping edges slightly. Layer half the sauce mixture and ⅓ of the cheese over tortillas; repeat layers, ending with tortillas. Spread tortillas with reserved sauce.

3. Bake 30 minutes, then top with remaining cheese and bake an additional 10 minutes or until sauce is bubbling and cheese is melted.

Makes 8 servings

Tip: Substitute refried beans for ground beef for a meatless main dish.

Prep Time: 10 minutes
Cook Time: 40 minutes

tip

Unopened packages of tortillas can be stored at room temperature, but any tortillas remaining in an open package should be wrapped and stored in the refrigerator.

mexican lasagna

PIZZA CASSEROLE

     2 cups uncooked rotini or other spiral pasta
 1½ pounds ground beef
     1 medium onion, chopped
        Salt and black pepper
     1 can (about 15 ounces) pizza sauce
     1 can (8 ounces) tomato sauce
     1 can (6 ounces) tomato paste
   ½ teaspoon sugar
   ½ teaspoon garlic salt
   ½ teaspoon dried oregano
     2 cups (8 ounces) shredded mozzarella cheese
 12 to 15 slices pepperoni

1. Preheat oven to 350°F. Cook pasta according to package directions; drain.

2. Meanwhile, cook beef and onion in large skillet over medium-high heat 6 to 8 minutes, stirring to break up meat. Drain fat. Season with salt and pepper.

3. Combine pasta, pizza sauce, tomato sauce, tomato paste, sugar, garlic salt and oregano in large bowl. Add beef mixture; stir until blended.

4. Place half of mixture in ovenproof skillet or 3-quart casserole; top with 1 cup cheese. Repeat layers. Arrange pepperoni slices on top.

5. Bake 25 to 30 minutes or until heated through and cheese is melted.

Makes 6 servings

TORTELLINI BAKE PARMESANO

    1 package (12 ounces) fresh or frozen cheese tortellini or ravioli
    ½ pound lean ground beef
    ½ medium onion, finely chopped
    2 cloves garlic, minced
    ½ teaspoon dried oregano, crushed
    1 can (26 ounces) DEL MONTE® Chunky Spaghetti Sauce with
        Garlic & Herb
    2 small zucchini, sliced
    ⅓ cup (about 1½ ounces) grated Parmesan cheese

1. Cook pasta according to package directions; rinse and drain.

2. Meanwhile, brown beef with onion, garlic and oregano in large skillet over medium-high heat; drain. Season with salt and pepper, if desired.

3. Add spaghetti sauce and zucchini. Cook 15 minutes or until thickened, stirring occasionally.

4. Arrange half of pasta in oiled 2-quart microwavable dish; top with half each of sauce and cheese. Repeat layers, ending with cheese; cover.

5. Microwave on HIGH 8 to 10 minutes or until heated through, rotating dish halfway through cooking time.   *Makes 4 servings*

Hint: For convenience, double the recipe and freeze one half for later use. The recipe can also be made ahead, refrigerated and heated just before serving (allow extra time in microwave if dish is chilled).

GARLIC MASHED POTATOES & BEEF BAKE

1 pound ground beef *or* ground turkey
1 can (10¾ ounces) CAMPBELL'S® Condensed Cream of Mushroom
    with Roasted Garlic Soup
1 tablespoon Worcestershire sauce
1 bag (16 ounces) frozen vegetables combination (broccoli, cauliflower,
    carrots), thawed
2 cups water
3 tablespoons butter
¾ cup milk
2 cups instant potato flakes *or* buds

1. Cook the beef in a 10-inch skillet over medium-high heat until the beef is well browned, stirring frequently to break up meat. Pour off any fat.

2. Stir the beef, **½ can** soup, Worcestershire and vegetables in a 12×8×2-inch shallow baking dish.

3. Heat the water, butter and remaining soup to a boil in a 2-quart saucepan over high heat. Remove from the heat. Stir in the milk. Slowly stir in the potatoes. Spoon potatoes over the beef mixture.

4. Bake at 400°F. for 20 minutes or until hot.   *Makes 4 servings*

Time-Saving Tip: To thaw vegetables, microwave on HIGH for 3 minutes.

CHILI BEEF AND CORN CASSEROLE

   ¾ **pound ground beef**
   ¼ **cup salsa**
   2 **teaspoons chili powder**
1½ **teaspoons ground cumin**
   2 **cups frozen corn, thawed**
   2 **ounces chopped collard greens, about ½-inch pieces (1 cup packed)**
   ½ **cup sour cream**
   ½ **cup (2 ounces) shredded sharp Cheddar cheese**

1. Preheat oven 350°F.

2. Brown beef in large skillet over medium-high heat, stirring to break up meat. Drain fat. Add salsa, chili powder and cumin; cook and stir 1 minute. Remove from heat.

3. Spray 8-inch square baking pan with cooking spray. Combine corn and collard greens in prepared pan. Spoon beef mixture evenly over vegetables; cover tightly with foil.

4. Bake 25 minutes or until greens are tender. Top each serving with sour cream and cheese.

Makes 4 servings

Collard greens are available at the supermarket throughout the year. Look for collard greens that have crisp leaves with no signs of yellowing. Store them in a plastic bag in the refrigerator for up to five days.

"

chili beef and corn casserole 63

POLKA DOT LASAGNA SKILLET

  1 pound ground beef
  1 package lasagna and sauce meal kit
  4 cups hot water
  ½ cup ricotta cheese
  1 egg
  3 tablespoons grated Parmesan cheese
  2 tablespoons all-purpose flour
  2 tablespoons chopped fresh parsley
  ½ teaspoon Italian seasoning
  ¼ teaspoon black pepper

1. Brown beef in large skillet over medium-high heat, stirring to break up meat. Drain fat.

2. Stir in contents of meal kit and hot water; bring to a boil. Reduce heat to low; cook, covered, 10 minutes.

3. Meanwhile, blend ricotta, egg, Parmesan, flour, parsley, Italian seasoning and pepper in small bowl until smooth.

4. Drop tablespoonfuls of ricotta mixture over pasta; cook, covered 4 to 5 minutes or until dumplings are set. Remove from heat; let stand about 4 minutes before serving. *Makes 4 to 6 servings*

HEARTY LASAGNA SOUP

      1 pound ground beef
    ¼ teaspoon garlic powder
    3½ cups SWANSON® Seasoned Beef Broth with Onion
      1 can (14.5 ounces) diced tomatoes, undrained
    ¼ teaspoon dried Italian seasoning, crushed
    1½ cups uncooked mini lasagna noodle-shaped pasta (mafalda)
          or corkscrew-shaped pasta (rotini)
    ¼ cup grated Parmesan cheese

1. Cook the beef with garlic in a 10-inch skillet over medium-high heat until well browned, stirring frequently to break up meat. Pour off any fat.

2. Stir the broth, tomatoes and Italian seasoning into the skillet. Heat to a boil.

3. Stir in the pasta. Reduce the heat to medium. Cook and stir for 10 minutes or until the pasta is tender but still firm. Stir in the cheese. Serve with additional cheese, if desired.   *Makes 4 servings*

Purchase Parmesan cheese in wedges from the supermarket and grate it yourself—it's less expensive than buying pre-shredded Parmesan, has better flavor and will last longer.

TACO–TOPPED POTATOES

    4 red or Yukon gold potatoes (about 6 ounces each), scrubbed and
        pierced with fork
 ½ pound ground beef
 ½ (1¼-ounce) package taco seasoning mix
 ½ cup water
  1 cup diced tomatoes
 ¼ teaspoon salt
  2 cups shredded lettuce
 ½ cup (2 ounces) shredded sharp Cheddar cheese
 ¼ cup finely chopped green onions
 ½ cup sour cream

1. Microwave potatoes on HIGH 6 to 7 minutes or until fork-tender.

2. Meanwhile, brown beef in medium skillet over medium-high heat, stirring to break up meat. Drain fat. Stir in seasoning mix and water; cook 1 minute. Remove from heat.

3. Combine tomatoes and salt in small bowl; mix gently.

4. Split potatoes almost in half and fluff with fork. Fill with equal amounts of beef mixture. Top with tomatoes, lettuce, cheese, green onions and sour cream. *Makes 4 servings*

BEEF WITH SNOW PEAS & BABY CORN

¾ pound ground beef
1 clove garlic, minced
1 teaspoon vegetable oil
6 ounces snow peas, halved lengthwise
1 red bell pepper, cut into strips
1 can (15 ounces) baby corn, drained and rinsed
1 tablespoon soy sauce
1 teaspoon sesame oil
  Salt and black pepper
2 cups cooked rice

1. Brown beef in large skillet over medium-high heat, stirring to break up meat. Drain fat. Add garlic; cook until tender. Transfer beef mixture to small bowl; set aside. Wipe out skillet with paper towel.

2. Heat vegetable oil in same skillet over medium-high heat. Add snow peas and bell pepper; cook and stir 2 to 3 minutes or until vegetables are crisp-tender. Stir in beef mixture, baby corn, soy sauce and sesame oil; cook until heated through. Season with salt and black pepper. Serve over rice. *Makes 4 servings*

UNSTUFFED PEPPERS

1 pound ground beef
1 jar (1 pound 10 ounces) RAGÚ® Old World Style® Traditional
    Pasta Sauce
2 large green and/or red bell peppers, coarsely chopped
1¼ cups water
1 cup instant rice

In 12-inch nonstick skillet, brown ground beef; drain, if desired. Stir in remaining ingredients. Bring to a boil over high heat. Reduce heat to medium-low and cook, covered, 20 minutes or until liquid is absorbed and rice is tender. *Makes 6 servings*

VEGGIE BEEF SKILLET SOUP

¾ pound ground beef
1 tablespoon olive oil
2 cups coarsely chopped cabbage
1 cup chopped green bell pepper
2 cups water
1 can (about 14 ounces) stewed tomatoes
1 cup frozen mixed vegetables
⅓ cup ketchup
1 tablespoon beef bouillon granules
2 teaspoons Worcestershire sauce
2 teaspoons balsamic vinegar
⅛ teaspoon red pepper flakes
¼ cup chopped fresh parsley

1. Brown beef in large skillet over medium-high heat, stirring to break up meat. Drain fat. Transfer beef to small bowl; set aside.

2. Heat oil in same skillet. Add cabbage and bell pepper; cook and stir 4 minutes or until cabbage is wilted. Add beef, water, tomatoes, mixed vegetables, ketchup, bouillon, Worcestershire sauce, vinegar and red pepper flakes; bring to a boil. Reduce heat to low; simmer, covered, 20 minutes.

3. Remove from heat; let stand 5 minutes. Stir in parsley before serving.
Makes 4 servings

veggie beef skillet soup

MEDITERRANEAN BEEF SKILLET

2½ cups (about 8 ounces) uncooked whole wheat rotini pasta
1 pound ground beef
½ teaspoon dried basil
½ teaspoon black pepper
1 can (about 14 ounces) diced tomatoes with garlic and onion
1 can (8 ounces) tomato sauce
1 bag (about 7 ounces) baby spinach, coarsely chopped
1 can (about 2 ounces) sliced black olives, drained
½ cup (2 ounces) crumbled herb-flavored feta cheese

1. Prepare pasta according to package directions; drain. Cover and keep warm.

2. Meanwhile, brown beef in large skillet over medium-high heat, stirring to break up meat. Drain fat. Stir in basil and pepper.

3. Add tomatoes, tomato sauce, spinach and olives; mix well. Cook over medium heat 10 minutes. Stir in reserved pasta; cook 5 minutes or until heated through. Sprinkle with cheese.   *Makes 4 servings*

If baby spinach is not available, regular spinach can be substituted. Swiss chard may also be used in the recipe; discard the stems and coarsely chop the leaves.

CHILI BEEF EXPRESS

   1 pound ground beef (95% lean)
   ¼ teaspoon salt
   ¼ teaspoon pepper
   1 can (15½ ounces) chili beans in chili sauce, undrained
   1 can (14½ ounces) chili-style chunky tomatoes, undrained
   1 cup frozen corn
   2 tablespoons chopped fresh cilantro

1. Brown ground beef in large nonstick skillet over medium heat 8 to 10 minutes or until beef is not pink, breaking up into ¾-inch crumbles. Pour off drippings; season with salt and pepper.

2. Stir in beans, tomatoes and corn; bring to a boil. Reduce heat; cover and simmer 10 minutes. Sprinkle with cilantro before serving.

Makes 4 servings (about 1¼ cups each)

Tip: This recipe may be doubled; you will need a Dutch oven to prepare it.

Prep and Cook Time: 25 minutes

Favorite recipe courtesy of *The Beef Checkoff*

BEEF TACO SKILLET

    1 pound ground beef
    1 can (10¾ ounces) CAMPBELL'S® Condensed Tomato Soup
    1 cup PACE® Chunky Salsa *or* Picante Sauce
    ½ cup water
    8 flour *or* corn tortillas (6 inches), cut into 1-inch pieces
    1 cup shredded Cheddar cheese

1. Cook the beef in a 10-inch skillet over medium-high heat until the beef is well browned, stirring to break up meat. Pour off any fat.

2. Stir the soup, salsa, water, tortillas and **half** the cheese into the skillet. Heat to a boil. Reduce the heat to low. Cover and cook for 5 minutes or until hot and bubbling.

3. Top with the remaining cheese.   *Makes 4 servings*

JAMBALAYA

    1 pound ground beef
    1 cup chopped onion
    ¼ cup diced green bell pepper
    1 can (28 ounces) tomatoes, liquid drained and reserved
    1 teaspoon salt
    ½ teaspoon sugar
    ¼ teaspoon dried thyme
    1 small bay leaf
  2⅓ cups cooked rice

1. Cook beef, onion and bell pepper in large skillet over medium-high heat 6 to 8 minutes, stirring to break up meat. Drain fat.

2. Add enough water to reserved tomato liquid to make 1½ cups. Add liquid, tomatoes, salt, sugar, thyme and bay leaf to skillet; simmer 5 minutes.

3. Stir in rice; simmer, covered, 5 minutes. Remove and discard bay leaf before serving.   *Makes 4 to 6 servings*

beef taco skillet

GROUND BEEF, SPINACH AND BARLEY SOUP

¾ pound ground beef
4 cups water
1 can (about 14 ounces) stewed tomatoes, undrained
1½ cups thinly sliced carrots
1 cup chopped onion
½ cup quick-cooking barley
1½ teaspoons beef bouillon granules
1½ teaspoons dried thyme
1 teaspoon dried oregano
½ teaspoon garlic powder
¼ teaspoon black pepper
⅛ teaspoon salt
3 cups torn stemmed spinach

1. Brown beef in large saucepan over medium-high heat, stirring to break up meat. Drain fat.

2. Stir in water, tomatoes with juice, carrots, onion, barley, bouillon, thyme, oregano, garlic powder, pepper and salt; bring to a boil over high heat. Reduce heat to medium-low; simmer, covered, 12 to 15 minutes or until barley and vegetables are tender, stirring occasionally.

3. Stir in spinach; cook just until spinach starts to wilt.

Makes 4 servings

ground beef, spinach and barley soup

CORN & ZUCCHINI MEDLEY

      ¾ pound ground beef
      1 package (10 ounces) frozen corn, thawed
      2 small zucchini (about 8 ounces), chopped
      1 large tomato, chopped
      ½ cup chopped onion
      1 teaspoon dried basil *or* 1 tablespoon chopped fresh basil
      ½ teaspoon dried thyme *or* 1½ teaspoons chopped fresh thyme
        Salt and black pepper

1. Brown beef in large skillet over medium-high heat, stirring to break up meat. Drain fat.

2. Reduce heat to medium-low. Stir in corn, zucchini, tomato, onion, basil and thyme. Cook, covered, 10 minutes or until zucchini is tender. Season with salt and pepper. *Makes 4 servings*

ITALIAN VEG•ALL® SKILLET

      1 pound ground beef
      1 can (15 ounces) VEG•ALL® Original Mixed Vegetables, drained
      1 jar (15½ ounces) prepared spaghetti sauce
      8 ounces uncooked pasta shells
      1 cup water
      1 cup tomato or vegetable juice
      ½ cup chopped onion
      1 tablespoon chopped parsley
      ½ teaspoon oregano
      ½ cup shredded Cheddar cheese

In large skillet, brown ground beef; drain thoroughly.

Add remaining ingredients except cheese. Bring to a boil. Cover, reduce heat and simmer 20 minutes, stirring occasionally.

Top with cheese. Cover; remove from heat. Let stand 5 minutes or until cheese melts. *Makes 4 to 6 servings*

SMOKEY CHILI WITH PASTA

2 cups (about 6 ounces) rotelle or rotini pasta, uncooked
1 pound ground beef
1 cup chopped onion
2 cans (about 15 ounces each) red kidney beans
2 cans (10¾ ounces each) condensed tomato soup
2 tablespoons HERSHEY'S Cocoa
2¼ teaspoons chili powder
¾ teaspoon ground black pepper
½ teaspoon salt
Grated Parmesan cheese (optional)

1. Cook pasta according to package directions; drain.

2. Meanwhile, cook ground beef and onion until meat is thoroughly done and onion is tender. If necessary, drain fat.

3. Stir in undrained kidney beans, soup, cocoa, chili powder, pepper and salt. Heat to boiling; reduce heat. Stir in hot pasta; heat thoroughly. Serve with Parmesan cheese, if desired. *Makes 8 servings*

slow cooker suppers

GRANDMA RUTH'S MINESTRONE

1 pound ground beef
1 cup dried red beans
1 package (16 ounces) frozen mixed vegetables
2 cans (8 ounces each) tomato sauce
1 can (about 14 ounces) diced tomatoes, undrained
¼ head shredded cabbage (about 2 cups)
1 cup chopped onion
1 cup chopped celery
½ cup chopped fresh parsley
1 tablespoon dried basil
1 tablespoon Italian seasoning
1 teaspoon salt
1 teaspoon black pepper
1 cup cooked macaroni

Slow Cooker Directions

1. Combine ground beef and beans in slow cooker. Cover; cook on HIGH 2 hours.

2. Add mixed vegetables, tomato sauce, tomatoes with juice, cabbage, onion, celery, parsley, basil, Italian seasoning, salt and pepper; stir to blend. Cover; cook on LOW 6 to 8 hours or until beans are tender.

3. Stir in macaroni. Cover; cook on HIGH 1 hour.   *Makes 4 servings*

CHIPOTLE TACO FILLING

2 pounds ground beef

2 cans (about 15 ounces each) pinto beans, rinsed and drained

2 cups chopped onions

1 can (about 14 ounces) diced tomatoes with peppers and onions, drained

2 chipotle peppers in adobo sauce, mashed

1 tablespoon beef bouillon granules

1 tablespoon sugar

1½ teaspoons ground cumin

Taco shells or flour tortillas

Shredded lettuce, salsa, shredded Mexican cheese blend and sour cream (optional)

Slow Cooker Directions

1. Brown beef in large skillet over medium-high heat, stirring to break up meat. Drain fat.

2. Combine beef, beans, onions, tomatoes, peppers, bouillon, sugar and cumin in slow cooker. Cover; cook on LOW 4 hours or on HIGH 2 hours.

3. Serve filling in taco shells. Top with lettuce, salsa, cheese and sour cream, if desired. *Makes 6 to 8 servings*

Chipotle chile peppers are typically found in small cans packed in adobo sauce, a mixture of chiles, herbs and vinegar. Chipotles are very hot, so a recipe rarely calls for more than one or two peppers. The remaining peppers can be refrigerated for up to several weeks or frozen for months. Blend or process the remaining peppers and sauce until smooth, then place the purée in small resealable food storage bags or plastic containers.

CLASSIC CHILI

1½ pounds ground beef
1½ cups chopped onions
 1 cup chopped green bell pepper
 2 cloves garlic, minced
 3 cans (about 15 ounces each) dark red kidney beans, rinsed and
    drained
 2 cans (about 15 ounces each) tomato sauce
 1 can (about 14 ounces) diced tomatoes, undrained
 2 to 3 teaspoons chili powder
 1 to 2 teaspoons dry hot mustard
 ¾ teaspoon dried basil
 ½ teaspoon black pepper
 1 to 2 dried hot chile peppers (optional)

Slow Cooker Directions

1. Cook beef, onions, bell pepper and garlic in large skillet over medium-high heat 6 to 8 minutes, stirring to break up meat. Drain fat. Transfer beef mixture to slow cooker.

2. Add beans, tomato sauce, tomatoes with juice, chili powder, mustard, basil, black pepper and chile peppers, if desired; mix well. Cover; cook on LOW 8 to 10 hours or on HIGH 4 to 5 hours.

3. Remove chile peppers before serving. *Makes 6 servings*

classic chili

91

CURRY BEEF

  1 pound ground beef
  1 medium onion, thinly sliced
  ½ cup beef broth
  1 tablespoon curry powder
  2 cloves garlic, minced
  1 teaspoon ground cumin
  1 cup sour cream
  ¼ cup milk
  ½ cup raisins, divided
  1 teaspoon sugar
  12 ounces uncooked wide egg noodles *or* 1⅓ cups uncooked long grain white rice
  ¼ cup chopped walnuts, almonds or pecans

Slow Cooker Directions

1. Brown beef in large skillet over medium-high heat, stirring to break up meat. Drain fat.

2. Transfer beef to slow cooker; stir in onion, broth, curry powder, garlic and cumin. Cover; cook on LOW 4 hours.

3. Stir in sour cream, milk, ¼ cup raisins and sugar. Cover; cook on LOW 30 minutes or until thickened and heated through.

4. Cook noodles according to package directions; drain. Spoon beef curry over noodles. Sprinkle with remaining ¼ cup raisins and walnuts.

Makes 4 servings

Serving Suggestion: Serve with sliced cucumber sprinkled with sugar and vinegar or plain yogurt topped with brown sugar, chopped bananas and green onions.

HAMBURGER SOUP

1 pound ground beef
1 cup thinly sliced carrots
1 cup sliced celery
1 package (1 ounce) dry onion soup mix
1 package (1 ounce) Italian salad dressing mix
¼ teaspoon seasoned salt
¼ teaspoon black pepper
3 cups boiling water
1 can (about 14 ounces) diced tomatoes, undrained
1 can (8 ounces) tomato sauce
1 tablespoon soy sauce
2 cups cooked macaroni
¼ cup grated Parmesan cheese
2 tablespoons chopped fresh parsley

Slow Cooker Directions

1. Brown beef in large skillet over medium-high heat, stirring to break up meat. Drain fat.

2. Place carrots and celery in slow cooker. Top with beef, soup mix, salad dressing mix, seasoned salt and pepper. Add water, tomatoes with juice, tomato sauce and soy sauce; mix well. Cover; cook on LOW 6 to 8 hours.

3. Stir in macaroni and cheese. Cover; cook on HIGH 15 to 30 minutes or until heated through. Sprinkle with parsley just before serving.

Makes 6 to 8 servings

BARLEY BEEF STROGANOFF

2½ cups reduced-sodium vegetable broth or water
⅔ cup uncooked pearl barley (not quick-cooking)
1 package (6 ounces) sliced mushrooms
½ teaspoon dried marjoram
½ teaspoon black pepper
½ pound ground beef
½ cup chopped celery
½ cup minced green onions
¼ cup half-and-half
Minced fresh parsley (optional)

Slow Cooker Directions

1. Place broth, barley, mushrooms, marjoram and pepper in slow cooker. Cover; cook on LOW 6 to 7 hours.

2. Brown beef in large skillet over medium-high heat, stirring to break up meat. Drain fat. Add celery and green onions; cook and stir 3 minutes.

3. Stir beef mixture and half-and-half into slow cooker mixture. Cover; cook on HIGH 10 to 15 minutes or until beef is hot and vegetables are tender. Sprinkle with parsley, if desired.   *Makes 4 servings*

Marjoram is a member of the mint family; it has a mild flavor similar to oregano. It is used frequently in Mediterranean cooking, particularly with meats and vegetables.

barley beef stroganoff

CHILI MAC IN THE SLOW COOKER

  1 pound ground beef
½ cup chopped onion
  1 can (about 14 ounces) diced tomatoes, drained
  1 can (8 ounces) tomato sauce
  2 tablespoons chili powder
  1 teaspoon garlic salt
½ teaspoon ground cumin
¼ teaspoon red pepper flakes
¼ teaspoon black pepper
  8 ounces uncooked elbow macaroni
    Shredded Cheddar cheese (optional)

Slow Cooker Directions

1. Cook beef and onion in large skillet over medium-high heat 6 to 8 minutes, stirring to break up meat. Drain fat.

2. Place beef mixture, tomatoes, tomato sauce, chili powder, garlic salt, cumin, red pepper flakes and black pepper in slow cooker; mix well. Cover; cook on LOW 4 hours.

3. Cook macaroni according to package directions until al dente; drain. Add macaroni to slow cooker; mix well. Cover; cook on LOW 1 hour. Serve with cheese, if desired. *Makes 4 to 6 servings*

SUZIE'S SLOPPY JOES

    3 pounds ground beef
    1 cup chopped onion
    3 cloves garlic, minced
 1¼ cups ketchup
    1 cup chopped red bell pepper
    ¼ cup plus 1 tablespoon Worcestershire sauce
    ¼ cup packed brown sugar
    3 tablespoons prepared mustard
    3 tablespoons cider vinegar
    2 teaspoons chili powder
      Toasted hamburger buns

Slow Cooker Directions

1. Cook beef, onion and garlic in large skillet over medium-high heat 6 to 8 minutes, stirring to break up meat. Drain fat.

2. Combine ketchup, pepper, Worcestershire sauce, brown sugar, mustard, vinegar and chili powder in slow cooker. Stir in beef mixture.

3. Cover; cook on LOW 6 to 8 hours. Spoon mixture onto hamburger buns.

Makes 8 servings

BROCCOLI AND BEEF PASTA

  2 cups broccoli florets *or* 1 package (10 ounces) frozen broccoli, thawed
  1 onion, thinly sliced
  ½ teaspoon dried basil
  ½ teaspoon dried oregano
  ½ teaspoon dried thyme
  1 can (about 14 ounces) Italian-style diced tomatoes, undrained
  ¾ cup beef broth
  1 pound ground beef
  2 cloves garlic, minced
  2 cups cooked rotini pasta
  ¾ cup (3 ounces) shredded Cheddar cheese or grated Parmesan cheese
  2 tablespoons tomato paste

Slow Cooker Directions

1. Layer broccoli, onion, basil, oregano, thyme, tomatoes with juice and broth in slow cooker. Cover; cook on LOW 2½ hours.

2. Cook beef and garlic in large skillet over medium-high heat 6 to 8 minutes, stirring to break up meat. Drain fat. Transfer beef mixture to slow cooker. Cover; cook on LOW 2 hours.

3. Stir in pasta, cheese and tomato paste. Cover; cook on LOW 30 minutes or until cheese melts and mixture is heated through. Sprinkle with additional cheese, if desired.   *Makes 4 servings*

Serving Suggestion: Serve with garlic bread.

WEEKNIGHT CHILI

 1 pound ground beef
 1 package (1¼ ounces) chili seasoning mix
 1 can (about 15 ounces) red kidney beans, rinsed and drained
 1 can (about 14 ounces) diced tomatoes with green chiles, undrained
 1 can (8 ounces) tomato sauce
 1 cup (4 ounces) shredded Cheddar cheese
   Sliced green onions (optional)

Slow Cooker Directions

1. Brown beef in large skillet over medium-high heat, stirring to break up meat. Drain fat. Stir in seasoning mix.

2. Place beef mixture, beans, tomatoes with juice and tomato sauce in slow cooker. Cover; cook on LOW 4 to 6 hours. Top each serving with cheese. Garnish with green onions.

Makes 4 servings

SLOW COOKER HAMBURGER CASSEROLE

 4 medium potatoes, thinly sliced
 3 carrots, thinly sliced
 1 can (15 ounces) green peas, drained
 1 can (15 ounces) corn, drained
 3 medium onions, chopped
 1½ pounds ground beef, browned and drained
   Salt and black pepper
 1 can (10¾ ounces) condensed tomato soup
 1 soup can water

Slow Cooker Directions

Place potatoes, carrots, peas, corn, onions and beef in slow cooker, occasionally seasoning with salt and pepper. Cover with tomato soup and water. Cover; cook on LOW 6 to 8 hours or on HIGH 3 to 4 hours.

Makes 6 servings

sandwiches & wraps

LEAN MEAN CHEESEBURGER

  1 pound ground beef (95% lean)
  2 tablespoons quick-cooking oats
  ½ teaspoon steak seasoning blend
  4 seeded *or* whole wheat hamburger buns, split
  4 slices low-fat cheese, such as Cheddar *or* American

Toppings:
    Lettuce leaves, tomato slices (optional)

1. Place oats in foodsafe plastic bag. Seal bag securely, squeezing out excess air. Roll over bag with rolling pin to crush oats to a fine consistency.

2. Combine ground beef, oats and steak seasoning blend in large bowl, mixing lightly but thoroughly. Lightly shape into four ½-inch patties.

3. Place patties on grid over medium, ash-covered coals. Grill, uncovered, 11 to 13 minutes to medium (160°F) doneness, until no longer pink in center and juices show no pink color, turning occasionally.

4. Line bottom of each bun with lettuce and tomato, if desired; top with burger and cheese slice. Close sandwiches.   *Makes 4 servings*

Prep and Cook Time: 20 minutes

Favorite recipe courtesy of *The Beef Checkoff*

SLOPPY JOE BURRITOS

    1 pound ground beef
    1 cup chopped bell pepper (red, green or a combination)
    ½ cup chopped onion
    1 can (16 ounces) sloppy joe sauce
    1 tablespoon cider vinegar
    1 teaspoon sugar
    1 teaspoon vegetable oil
    ¼ teaspoon salt
    2 cups coleslaw mix
    4 (7- to 8-inch) colored tortilla wraps

1. Cook beef, pepper and onion in large skillet over medium-high heat 6 to 8 minutes, stirring to break up meat. Drain fat. Stir in sloppy joe sauce; cook over low heat about 3 minutes or until slightly thickened.

2. Whisk vinegar, sugar, oil and salt in medium bowl until well blended. Add coleslaw mix; toss to coat.

3. Divide beef mixture evenly among tortillas. Top with ½ cup coleslaw mix. Roll up tortillas burrito style, folding in sides to enclose filling.

Makes 4 servings

The largest container of vegetable oil at the grocery store may seem like a bargain, but think about how much you use before making that purchase. Oil can turn rancid after being stored for several months, so if you don't use it frequently, you might end up throwing much of it away—and then you'll be throwing away money along with the oil.

sloppy joe burrito

109

QUICK GREEK PITAS

    1 pound ground beef
    1 package (10 ounces) frozen chopped spinach, thawed
        and well drained
    4 green onions, chopped
    1 can (2¼ ounces) sliced black olives, drained
    1 teaspoon dried oregano, divided
    ¼ teaspoon black pepper
    1 large tomato, diced
    1 cup plain yogurt
    ½ cup mayonnaise
    6 (6-inch) pita breads, warmed
      Lettuce leaves
    1 cup (4 ounces) crumbled feta cheese

1. Brown beef in large skillet over medium-high heat, stirring to break up meat. Drain fat.

2. Stir in spinach, green onions, olives, ½ teaspoon oregano and pepper; cook and stir 2 minutes. Stir in tomato.

3. Combine yogurt, mayonnaise and remaining ½ teaspoon oregano in small bowl.

4. Split open pita breads; line each with lettuce leaf. Stir cheese into beef mixture; divide among pita pockets. Serve with yogurt sauce.

Makes 6 servings

RAGÚ® PIZZA BURGERS

    1 pound ground beef
    2 cups RAGÚ® Old World Style® Pasta Sauce, divided
    1 cup shredded mozzarella cheese (about 4 ounces), divided
    ¼ teaspoon salt
    6 English muffins, split and toasted

1. In small bowl, combine ground beef, ½ cup Ragú Pasta Sauce, ½ cup cheese and salt. Shape into 6 patties. Grill or broil until done.

2. Meanwhile, heat remaining pasta sauce. Arrange burgers on muffin halves. Top with remaining cheese and sauce.   *Makes 6 servings*

CHILI CORN WRAPS

    4 large flour tortillas
    1 tablespoon vegetable oil
    1 medium onion, chopped
    1 green bell pepper, diced
    1 pound lean ground beef or turkey
    2 tablespoons TABASCO® brand Green Jalapeño Pepper Sauce
    1 tablespoon chili powder
    1 teaspoon salt
    1 (11-ounce) can corn, drained
    1 (4-ounce) jar diced pimientos, drained
    ½ cup (2 ounces) shredded Monterey Jack cheese

Preheat oven to 375°F. Wrap tortillas in foil; heat 10 minutes. Heat oil in 12-inch skillet over medium heat. Add onion and bell pepper; cook 5 minutes or until tender-crisp. Remove vegetables with slotted spoon.

Add beef to drippings remaining in skillet; cook over medium-high heat until well browned, stirring occasionally. Stir in TABASCO® Green Sauce, chili powder and salt; cook 1 minute, stirring frequently. Remove from heat. Stir in vegetable mixture, corn, pimientos and Monterey Jack cheese. To assemble wraps, place ¼ of mixture on each tortilla; roll up tortillas, tucking in sides.   *Makes 4 servings*

ragú® pizza burger

NOT–SO–SLOPPY JOES

    1 pound ground beef
 ⅓ cup finely chopped onion
 ⅓ cup shredded carrot
    1 can (8 ounces) tomato sauce, divided
    1 egg
 ½ teaspoon salt
 ½ teaspoon Italian seasoning
 ⅛ teaspoon black pepper
    6 hot dog buns
    6 slices mozzarella cheese, halved

1. Preheat oven to 350°F. Spray 13×9-inch baking pan with nonstick cooking spray.

2. Combine beef, onion, carrot, ½ can (4 ounces) tomato sauce, egg, salt, Italian seasoning and pepper in large bowl; mix lightly. Shape beef mixture into 1½-inch balls. Place meatballs in prepared pan; top with remaining ½ can tomato sauce.

3. Bake 15 to 20 minutes or until meatballs are browned and heated through. Remove from oven; cover to keep warm.

4. Meanwhile, open buns and arrange on baking sheet. Place 2 cheese halves on bottom of each bun. Heat buns about 7 minutes or until cheese begins to melt. Spoon meatballs into each bun.

Makes 6 servings

BEEF & SALSA BURRITOS

  1¼ pounds ground beef
  1½ tablespoons chili powder
   ½ teaspoon salt
   ½ teaspoon ground cumin
   ¼ teaspoon pepper
   1 package (10 ounces) frozen chopped spinach, defrosted, drained well
  1¼ cups prepared chunky salsa
   1 cup shredded Cheddar cheese
   8 medium flour tortillas (8-inch diameter), warmed

1. Brown ground beef in large nonstick skillet over medium heat 8 to 10 minutes or until beef is not pink, breaking up into small crumbles. Pour off drippings; season with chili powder, salt, cumin and pepper.

2. Stir in spinach and salsa; heat through. Remove from heat; stir in cheese.

3. Spoon about ½ cup beef mixture down center of each tortilla, leaving 1½-inch border at bottom. Fold bottom edge up over filling. Fold right and left sides to center, overlapping edges.

Makes 4 servings

Favorite recipe courtesy of **The Beef Checkoff**

SPINACH & FETA BURGERS

   2 pounds ground beef
   ½ cup water
   4 ounces feta cheese, crumbled
   1 package KNORR® Cream of Spinach Recipe Mix
   1 tablespoon finely chopped garlic

In large bowl, combine all ingredients; shape into 8 patties. Grill or broil until done. Serve, if desired, on rolls with lettuce and tomato.

Makes 8 servings

beef & salsa burritos

WILD WEST PICANTE BURGERS

  1 pound ground beef
  ½ cup PACE® Picante Sauce *or* Chunky Salsa
  4 hamburger rolls, split

1. Thoroughly mix the beef and picante sauce in a medium bowl. Shape the mixture into 4 (½-inch-thick) burgers.

2. Lightly oil the grill rack and heat the grill to medium. Grill the burgers for 10 minutes for medium* or until desired doneness, turning the burgers over halfway through cooking and brushing them often with additional picante sauce while cooking.

3. Serve the burgers in the rolls with additional picante sauce.

Makes 4 sandwiches

The internal temperature of the burgers should reach 160°F.

TACOS OLÉ

  1 pound ground beef or turkey
  1 cup salsa
  ¼ cup *Frank's® RedHot®* Original Cayenne Pepper Sauce
  2 teaspoons ground chili powder
  8 taco shells, heated
  1⅓ cups *French's®* French Fried Onions

1. Cook beef in skillet over medium-high heat until browned; drain. Stir in salsa, **Frank's RedHot** Sauce and chili powder. Heat to boiling. Reduce heat; cook 5 minutes, stirring often.

2. To serve, spoon meat mixture into taco shells. Top with French Fried Onions. Splash on more **Frank's RedHot** Sauce to taste. Garnish as desired.

Makes 4 servings

wild west picante burger

PICADILLO TACOS

  6 ounces ground beef
½ cup chopped green bell pepper
½ teaspoon ground cumin
½ teaspoon chili powder
⅛ teaspoon ground cinnamon
½ cup chunky salsa
  1 tablespoon golden raisins
  4 (6-inch) corn tortillas, warmed
½ cup shredded lettuce
  1 small tomato, chopped
¼ cup (1 ounce) shredded Cheddar cheese

1. Combine beef, pepper, cumin, chili powder and cinnamon in large skillet. Cook over medium-high heat 4 to 6 minutes, stirring to break up meat. Drain fat. Add salsa and raisins; reduce heat and simmer 5 minutes, stirring occasionally.

2. Serve beef mixture in tortillas; top with lettuce, tomato and cheese.

Makes 2 servings

NEW ORLEANS BURGERS

  1 pound lean ground beef
¼ cup thinly sliced green onions, including tops
1½ teaspoons LAWRY'S® Garlic Salt
¾ teaspoon dried basil
½ teaspoon dried thyme
½ teaspoon hot pepper sauce

In large bowl, combine all ingredients. Shape mixture into 4 patties. Grill or broil until thoroughly cooked, about 4 to 6 minutes per side.

Makes 4 servings

Serving Suggestion: Serve on lightly toasted onion rolls with grilled onions.

picadillo tacos

FRENCH ONION BURGERS

1 pound ground beef
1 can (10½ ounces) CAMPBELL'S® Condensed French Onion Soup
4 slices cheese
4 round hard rolls, split

1. Shape the beef into 4 (½-inch-thick) burgers.

2. Heat a 10-inch skillet over medium-high heat. Add the burgers and cook until well browned on both sides. Remove the burgers and set aside. Pour off any fat.

3. Stir the soup into the skillet. Heat to a boil. Return the burgers to the skillet and reduce the heat to low. Cover and cook for 5 minutes or until the burgers are cooked through.* Top with cheese and continue cooking until the cheese melts. Serve burgers in rolls with soup mixture for dipping.

Makes 4 burgers

**The internal temperature of the burgers should reach 160°F.*

Shape the burgers a day ahead, then cover and refrigerate them to make mealtime quicker. Or, purchase burgers already shaped at your local supermarket.

GRANDE BEEF EMPANADA

    1 pound ground beef
    ¼ cup raisins, chopped
    ¼ cup chili sauce
    1 teaspoon ground cumin
    ¼ teaspoon salt
    ¼ teaspoon pepper
    1 refrigerated pie crust (½ of 15-ounce package)
    Water

Toppings:

    Salsa con queso, prepared salsa, chopped fresh cilantro

1. Heat oven to 400°F. Brown ground beef in large nonstick skillet over medium heat 8 to 10 minutes or until beef is not pink, breaking into small crumbles. Pour off drippings.

2. Stir in raisins, chili sauce, cumin, salt and pepper. Cook and stir 1 minute. Remove from heat.

3. Unfold pie crust; place on baking sheet. Spoon beef mixture evenly over ½ of dough, leaving 1½-inch border around edge. Moisten edge of dough with water; fold pastry over filling. Press edges of dough together with fork to seal. Prick center of dough with fork once or twice to form steam vents.

4. Bake in 400°F oven 16 to 18 minutes or until pastry is golden brown. Serve with toppings, if desired.

Makes 4 servings

Beef Empanada Appetizers: Increase refrigerated pie crusts to 3 *or* 1½ (15-ounce) packages. Prepare ground beef filling as above. Roll out each pie crust to a 14-inch circle on a lightly floured surface. Cut 10 circles from each crust with a 3½-inch round cookie or biscuit cutter, spacing the cutouts closely. Spoon a generous tablespoon beef filling in center of each circle, leaving ¼-inch border around edge. Moisten edge of dough with water; fold pastry over filling to form half-circle. Press edge together with fork to seal. Place on baking sheet. Bake in 400°F oven 14 to 16 minutes or until pastry is golden brown. Serve as above. Makes 30 appetizers.

Favorite recipe courtesy of *The Beef Checkoff*

ACKNOWLEDGEMENTS

The publisher would like to thank the companies and organizations listed below for the use of their recipes and photographs in this publication.

Courtesy of The Beef Checkoff

Campbell Soup Company

Del Monte Corporation

The Hershey Company

McIlhenny Company (TABASCO® brand Pepper Sauce)

Ortega®, A Division of B&G Foods, Inc.

Reckitt Benckiser Inc.

Riviana Foods Inc.

Unilever

Veg•All®

METRIC CONVERSION CHART

VOLUME MEASUREMENTS (dry)

1/8 teaspoon = 0.5 mL
1/4 teaspoon = 1 mL
1/2 teaspoon = 2 mL
3/4 teaspoon = 4 mL
1 teaspoon = 5 mL
1 tablespoon = 15 mL
2 tablespoons = 30 mL
1/4 cup = 60 mL
1/3 cup = 75 mL
1/2 cup = 125 mL
2/3 cup = 150 mL
3/4 cup = 175 mL
1 cup = 250 mL
2 cups = 1 pint = 500 mL
3 cups = 750 mL
4 cups = 1 quart = 1 L

VOLUME MEASUREMENTS (fluid)

1 fluid ounce (2 tablespoons) = 30 mL
4 fluid ounces (1/2 cup) = 125 mL
8 fluid ounces (1 cup) = 250 mL
12 fluid ounces (1 1/2 cups) = 375 mL
16 fluid ounces (2 cups) = 500 mL

WEIGHTS (mass)

1/2 ounce = 15 g
1 ounce = 30 g
3 ounces = 90 g
4 ounces = 120 g
8 ounces = 225 g
10 ounces = 285 g
12 ounces = 360 g
16 ounces = 1 pound = 450 g

DIMENSIONS

1/16 inch = 2 mm
1/8 inch = 3 mm
1/4 inch = 6 mm
1/2 inch = 1.5 cm
3/4 inch = 2 cm
1 inch = 2.5 cm

OVEN TEMPERATURES

250°F = 120°C
275°F = 140°C
300°F = 150°C
325°F = 160°C
350°F = 180°C
375°F = 190°C
400°F = 200°C
425°F = 220°C
450°F = 230°C

BAKING PAN SIZES

Utensil	Size in Inches/Quarts	Metric Volume	Size in Centimeters
Baking or	8 × 8 × 2	2 L	20 × 20 × 5
Cake Pan	9 × 9 × 2	2.5 L	23 × 23 × 5
(square or	12 × 8 × 2	3 L	30 × 20 × 5
rectangular)	13 × 9 × 2	3.5 L	33 × 23 × 5
Loaf Pan	8 × 4 × 3	1.5 L	20 × 10 × 7
	9 × 5 × 3	2 L	23 × 13 × 7
Round Layer	8 × 1½	1.2 L	20 × 4
Cake Pan	9 × 1½	1.5 L	23 × 4
Pie Plate	8 × 1¼	750 mL	20 × 3
	9 × 1¼	1 L	23 × 3
Baking Dish	1 quart	1 L	—
or Casserole	1½ quart	1.5 L	—
	2 quart	2 L	—